Losing Myself Brought Me Here

By Jennae Cecelia

Cover art by Islam Farid
www.IslamFarid.net
Instagram: @islamsfarid

Cecelia's Diner logo by Mariah
Danielsen of Wander Design Co.
www.wanderdesignco.com
Instagram: @wanderdesignco

ISBN: 9781099275319

This book is a work of fiction. Names,
characters, places, and incidents are
products of the author's imagination or
are used factiously. Any resemblance to
actual events of locales or persons,
living or dead is entirely
coincidental.

For Loren,

My number one supporter, best friend, and love of my life. I am thankful every single day that you told me, "you should write a book" after I talked about all the poetry I had created.

Seven books later and I could not have done it without you. At least not in the same way.

Getting lost brought me to you. <3

*A book filled with words
written while wandering.*

Dear Reader,

*Getting lost is part of the journey.
Whether you are in high school and
unsure where you fit in, or in
college and do not know where you
are going to go next.
Maybe you are working at a job you
do not like but need.
Or perhaps you are lost in a
relationship with a significant
other, family member, or friend.
Whatever it may be, we all get lost
at times, but it is what we learn
from being lost that helps us
through this journey called life.*

*This is my journey from being so
completely lost in life, to finding
the roads that lead me to where I
want to go. Although I have found my
way I still get lost at times. I go
on detours, make pit stops, and hit
dead ends, but I have learned to
embrace the ride.*

Come with me on my road trip.

*Love,
Jennae*

I walked into a diner in between
where I was from and where I was
going.
The waitress made her way to the
stool I precisely chose at the
counter hoping no one would sit on
either side of me, but also hoping
someone would.
When she got to my seat she asked
what brought me into that old diner
with the neon signs & delicious pie,
and I looked her straight in the eye
and said, "Losing myself did."

TABLE NO.
PERSONS
1
CHECK NO.
2363-18
BEV • APPET • SOUP/SALAD • ENTREE • VEG • DESSERT
1 coffee
1 slice apple pie
GETTING
LOST

Sit me by an ocean.
Five dollars to my name.
As I look out at an endless wave
coming at me,
I contemplate how things
got this way.
Two dollars to fill up my gas tank
one gallon and drive *maybe* 20
miles more.
One dollar to get a gas station
coffee,
I am eager to pour.
Two dollars left to last me until
I have found what I am searching
for.
Sit me by an ocean so I can ask,
"When will all of this be better?
When will this be the past that I
can look back on and write a thank
you letter."

HOW DO I BLOCK OUT
THE WORDS TRYING TO
MAKE ME FEEL DEFEATED?
HOW DO I TELL THEM THAT
GETTING TO THIS DREAM
WAS ALL I
EVER NEEDED?

I was not invited to
the after-parties,
pool parties,
or sit around and linger
awkwardly parties.
Not that I wanted to go anyways.
Not that I would even fit in.
Because no one is looking to talk
about the stars,
the moon,
or why we even exist.

I sat at home on Friday nights
and made Spotify playlists
that reflected my mood.
I laid around on Saturday evenings
and binged watched Netflix
until half past two.
I sat at home and thought about
all the things that I
wanted to be doing.
But my homebody self
with social anxiety
preferred to live
vicariously through the
people in those movies.

They hate me.

They are mad at me.

They hate me.

They are mad at me.

Why did I say that?

Why did I do that?

Do they hate me?

Are they mad at me?

Oh wait, they messaged back.

No, *"haha"* or *"LOL."*

They only said, *"Sounds good."*

So all must be well,

right?

Or are they mad at me?

-what my anxiety makes me think

He said,
*"You are a happy,
good girl."*
But what he did not know
was I was just a girl
who was good at
pretending to be happy
when I was really not.

I do not know why
you can not be happy
that I want to
pave my own way.
You always said that you
wanted better for me,
but I guess what you
REALLY meant
was as long as our
versions of better
were the same.

This lifestyle is
not sustainable.
It may work for a while,
but long term the pieces
will crumble apart.
Fighting back tears will only
end in a flood.
Saying, *"I am okay"* will start to
sound like a broken record
with a scratch.
This lifestyle is not sustainable.
It is time to get back on track
with being honest to myself about
how long this can really last.
How long I can act like
everything is bringing me
happiness.

I never gave myself
the love that I deserved
when walking through
the high school halls.
I heard people gossiping
between the bell.
I feared they would not like
me as well.
But the truth was,
I did not even like myself.
I was talking behind my own back.
I was my own fake friend.

I fall in love with places
that have importance,
so why am I still struggling
to fall in love
with the body
I have always called home?

Here I am.
Out dancing and sipping my drink.
Then I look over my shoulder,
and there is Anxiety.
Walking through the door
like an ex-boyfriend I do not
want to see.
With a big grin ready to greet me.
Go away! I think.
All you do is cause me pain.
Yet my voice goes silent
before I can say the words.
So here I am sitting in the booth
waiting for Anxiety to leave a
party they were never invited to.

As I poured my cup of coffee out
of our ten-dollar coffee maker,
he asked me how
I was feeling today.
I looked into
the cup of darkness
in front of me,
brought it to my lips,
and took a sip with caution.
"I am good." I said.
As good as cheap coffee can be.

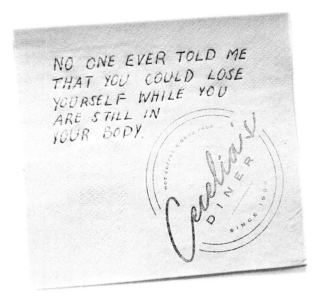

What would it feel like
to let fear free?
Send it off into the wind
like a balloon with a string
that I am not eager to reach.
What would it feel like
to let fear go?
Throw it out in a bottle
into the ocean of unknown.

I am afraid to make
the drive back home,
to where people and places
expect something from me.
Unlike the wide-open road and
strangers in coffee shops,
who only care that I am
appreciating the view
and chatting about
what brought me here.
I am afraid to make
the drive back home
because I am not sure if
it is even home
or just a place that
I have grown
uncomfortably
comfortable in.

I am alone in the most
crowded places.
Around familiar
or unfamiliar faces.
I am alone in this
big city.
How am I alone
even when many people
are with me?

I do not know how to cry for you,
and it is not because
I do not care.
I do not know how to cry for you,
because I do not even know
how to cry for myself.

I want to be as transparent as the
rain dripping down a window
reflecting who I am inside.

Life is a road trip with
no guaranteed destination.
No exact directions.
No knowledge of how long
it will last.
Life is a road trip that can
have adventure and conflicts.
But it is a trip worth taking
with the most open mind you can.

I wish you knew that even though
I keep a straight face
as you talk down to me.
Tell me I am flawed.
That I will not succeed.
There are still tears there even
if you can not see them.
The bite marks on the inside of
my cheeks speak my pain.

Sometimes I feel like
one of the last leaves
clinging to the tree
in early winter.
Barely hanging on
when the weather should have
already taken me down.

I HAD TO LET YOU GO
AND IT WAS NOT
ANYTHING YOU DID.
IT ██ WAS
WHAT I COULD
NOT DO
FOR MYSELF.

Cecelia's
DINER
HOT COFFEE & GOOD FOOD
SINCE 1994

It was like swallowing
cough syrup.
Not knowing if it was going to be
the cherry flavor that was
surprisingly good,
or the kind that tasted
like grass.
That is how I felt every time
I answered your call,
never knowing what version
I was going to get.

I aspire to be
more like the older man
sitting next to me
in this diner.
Doing his crossword puzzle
in peace.
No sight of an
electronic device
to take his mind
to another place,
other than **here,**
right now,
with his coffee,
paper,
and the breeze.

Will today be the day that
everything changes?
Things can not possibly
get worse,
can they?
Because I know I hit rock bottom
so that must mean
things can only get better.
But what if my rock bottom
just keeps moving locations
and I am in rock bottom forever?

You say that it seems like
I have the strength
of tall ocean waves.
But what you do not know
is that I am holding back
what feels like
ocean waves,
and I do not know
how much longer
I can keep up with
this constant force.

I think I have grown
too comfortable with
getting another tomorrow.
So much so that
I waste today.
I think I have grown
too comfortable with
being guaranteed something that
was never even promised to me.
So why am I waiting
for the clock to
strike six in the morning
to make today the day
I go after what I have
always wanted?
And if by eight
it has not happened,
well there is that friend
tomorrow again.
That friend I can not
always rely on.

When there was
nothing on the line,
I could dream just fine.
But when the responsibilities
built-up more and more.
Starting at my toes
and now my throat.
It is hard for me to dream
when the weight of
responsibility is
burying me.

What would it look like
to do more than just survive?
Would I say yes to more?
Would I effortlessly start up
conversations with random
strangers?
Would I paint that picture
or write the book that
I have been scared
to put out there?
Would I leave the job I hate
because I am only there
for the check it provides?
What would it look like
to do more than just survive?
What would it feel like
to be truly alive?

I will stay for one more drink
but I will probably just
leave it sitting on the bar
collecting a condensation ring.
I do not actually want
one more drink,
I just do not want
this night to end.
I am afraid of the morning
when I have to face
reality again.

You welcomed me in
from the cold
with open arms,
blankets,
coffee,
and the fire
ready to greet me.
But your smile is what really
made me feel warm and welcomed.
It is not the materialistic
things I need.
I just would really enjoy
genuine company.

What if people find out that
the girl they call
so happy and
put together,
is really just a mess
with her own bad weather.

I wish you would listen to what my story actually is before you start writing the version you think it should be.

You tell me that you never knew
I felt that way,
but you never even asked me
how I was doing.
How can you know how I feel
if you do not ask?
You can not just go based off
what you see on the surface.

People would call me calm like a
slow breeze on a Sunday afternoon.
Little did they know my mind was
always feeling like a typhoon.
I hid my weather well.

You said, *"I do not understand why
you are so upset when I cancel
plans last minute."*
I get so upset because
I have already played it
over and over in my mind.
Exhausting every situation
that could happen.
Now all that time is
wasted even more
because it
is not happening.

I am a house with no windows.
I do not want anyone to see in.
I do not want to feel vulnerable.
But soon I learned that I was
missing out on beautiful views.
If I have no windows
people can not see in,
but I can not see out.

I have to swim.
I have to swim.
But I am scared of how long
I will have to keep moving
and moving
before I can
take a break.
Before I can conquer
these monstrous waves.

I was not lost or found.
I was a bit in the middle.
I was afraid to find out too much
about myself but I did not want to
be misplaced either.

THE PAST CAN ONLY
COME BACK IN MY MIND.
KIND OF LIKE YOU.

Tell me your coming home story.
All the faces eager to see you.
Tell me how they missed you.
Tell me, how did you feel?
Because when I came home,
no one even noticed.
There was no one at the airport
holding up a sign.
Maybe it was because when I came
home it was me feeling at home
deep inside.
No one may have noticed my
absence,
but I sure felt it.

I want the friend that will
invite me over mid-afternoon
for coffee and conversation
to fill the room.
I am tired of friends who make me
feel like I am an afterthought.
Only reaching out to me for
company when everyone else on
their list either
could not come or forgot.

The thing I fear the most
is not getting to do
all the things I truly would
like to do if fear did not
live in my mind.
Like riding a bike down the road
in a European city.
Or swim in the ocean of unknown
with no one else with me.
Or simply just leave my home
to walk through the woods alone
and not fear if someone is
following behind creepily.

Drive to the airport.
Spontaneously pick a flight.
Take that risk.
You have nothing but time.
Go places you only saw
happening in your mind.
Bring only what you really need.
Leave what is weighing heavy on
your mind behind.

I am lost amongst the wildflowers.
Waiting for my sun to rise.
I know it is coming soon.

This road may not end on the
destination you had
set out to go to.
This road may end at a place
you think has no meaning.
But the memories you make here
and the footprints you leave,
will help you realize it is the
place you did not even know
you needed.

Do not invite me over for dinner
to pick me apart
the same way I am picking
at the food staring at me
on my plate.
You can not say anything to me
that is worse than what I have
already said to myself today.

I am trying to make
my safe place
my own arms.
I am tired of running
to places I think are safe,
but are really just a trap.

"I will not be there today. I am taking time to myself. My self-care comes first."

What I want to send out in a mass text, but would anyone truly understand that I am not actually ditching them?

I wonder if I will
still mean
the confident things
I said at 1:00 a.m.
when 9:00 a.m. comes
and makes me
feel embarrassed
for being so bold.

I wish I could go back home and
pretend that I was new in town.
Greet the people I have
always known like it is
our first go around.
Appreciate the views
I have looked past so often.
I wish I could go back home and
not have to proceed with caution.

Is this destination really
the *end* of a journey
or is it just the *beginning*
of the next one?

Sometimes I hold my tears in
for so long that when
the woman at
the check out line asks,
"How are you today?"
She now becomes
the therapist
I could not afford.
"Not good."
Tears rolling down my cheeks.
She looks at me like
she wants to say something.
please anything
But instead, she scans
my chocolate
and sour candy,
hands me the receipt
and says,
"Have a nice day."

-Just another person
ignoring my pain

I fear being on
this earth for
30,
50,
or 80 years
and never doing what
fulfills my soul.
I fear waking up
and realizing
that this was not
what I wanted for myself
and not knowing
where to turn.

I know what I deserve
and it is not just a,
"Hello"
when *you* need something.
Only to be ignored
every moment *I* need something.
If you want a response from me,
you can no longer only call
when you are in need and you know
I am the only one who will answer.
Do not take advantage of the fact
that I care too much.

I got comfortable in the heart
that used to beat in your chest.
But now that you have changed,
I am lost in a heart
that I want to get out of.
But I can not seem to
find a way to escape.

I have been a victim of,
"Here you go,
wait never mind,
give it back."
I no longer get my hopes up
because I fear it is a trap.
Getting my hopes up
and then feeling
the first big drop of
the roller coaster
going down.

I may not be the easiest
person to love,
but trust me when I say
that the only reason
I am not easy to love
is because in
the back of my mind
I fear you going away.

If you had to let the supportive
people in your life go today,
would you still be able to
hold yourself up on your own?

Throw the map into the backseat.
Put your phone on airplane mode.
Just enjoy the ride.
Wherever you may go.

I AM CLINGING TO THE
SUNSETS I REMEMBER
COMING AT THE END OF
THE DAY. TO REMIND ME
OF ALL THE BEAUTY
I FORGOT TO
NOTICE ALONG
THE WAY.

I **want to be** the friend that
checks in and asks you
how you are doing daily.
I **want to be** the friend that
keeps track of all the events
happening in your life.
I **want to be** the friend who
reminds you about all the
amazing things you are doing.
I **want to be** that friend,
and I am trying to be that
for myself too.

No matter how many times
I think I have found who I am,
there is always
a shift eventually.
Big or small.
For the good or for the bad.
I know I can not stay
one constant person.
That is what growing really is.

There are memories
I want to forget.
Pack away in a box
that will only collect dust.
Leave abandoned in a house
I no longer go to.
But no matter how many times
I hide them
they still find a way
to pop back up.

I saw all the caution signs
and the ones that
kept telling me to
turn around.
I ignored all the signs
right in front of me,
and then blamed the Universe
for trying to take me down
with no warning.

You may feel the most lost
in a place that should
feel like home.
You may feel the most at home
in a place you barely know.
Maybe it is time to wander to
somewhere new.
Hit the road and go.

I stopped getting wrapped up
in the idea that I had to
figure out who I was exactly.
I put the label maker down.
So should you.
Not just when it comes to
labeling yourself
but stop sticking your labels
on other people too.

I feel like the hitchhiker
no one wants to pick up
along the way.
Although they look at me in
concern and appear to be thinking
about if they should stop,
I can tell they are too worried
about what they have to do today.

I can hit the road
and pack my suitcase
as tight as can be.
Not able to fit
even one more thing.
But anxiety always seems
to find a way to squeeze into
the extra cracks
in between everything.
That is anxiety for you,
never letting me leave alone.
Not even allowing a moment
for me to just breathe.

I am sorry I am always leaving.
I am afraid to plant my roots
too deep in the ground.
Because uprooting myself after
being planted for so long
involves more and more
people each time around.

I am trying to see the beauty
in what is here for me right now.
Instead of only seeing the beauty
in things I long for but
have never even held.

I have a hard time finishing
anything because endings are not
easy for me to embrace.
I do not want things to end.
I want to be able to
look forward to it each day.

At one point we were strangers who
only knew each other's faces
and it was better that way.
Then we got to know each other and
when it was time to let go,
you were no longer just a face,
you were one of the only people
that felt like home.
I did not want to lose my home.
Please do not evict me
from your life.
Because now I am wishing when we
saw each other we did not say hi.

*-all of your hellos lead to
goodbyes*

I am known for
picking flower petals
off the ground
and wishing I could help them
get back on the plant
where they belong.
I am known for
trying to help
everyone else
but myself.

Every time I was hot summer,
you wanted cool autumn.
And every time I was
cozy autumn,
you wanted adventurous summer.
Instead of prematurely
changing seasons
I told you I was just not
your weather.

I am on a journey.
No GPS set.
No map.
Just looking for rest.
A place to make mends
with my mind.
A journey to reset.

A pine tree
is always a pine tree
and I do not think
anyone realizes how much
I crave the consistency of
knowing what I always am.

-thoughts in the woods

I tell you that I
do not care.
I care.
That I do not miss you.
I miss you.
That you mean
nothing to me anymore.
You mean everything to me.
If you read between the lines all
of those words hint at a girl who
is still not over why you left her
that Thursday evening
at your door.
She is trying to act like
what you did,
did not hurt her
but it did.
It hurt.
And thinking about it now
hurts even more.

I showed up with my hair in a
messy bun.
My shoelaces undone.
Acne scars lingering on my face.
Tear streaks permanently
staining my cheeks.
And all I could think about
was what people might be saying
about how I look.
Then a girl sat down a few tables
from me and I heard her apologize
for looking **"rough"** to the guy
she was meeting.
But her blue eyes shined.
Her smile was big and eager to
make someone happy.
In that moment I wanted to tell
her how beautiful she was.
That I was not looking at her hair
in a bun or her outfit.
I was looking at someone who
embodied love.
Then I realized maybe someone out
there has thought the same about
me, while I was calling myself
"rough."

There is something so freeing
about sharing your soul
with people who have
no expectations about
who you should be
or where you should go.

I let you tell me
who I was for so long
that I started to think
I was your shadow.
And you did too.
You did not want a best friend,
you just wanted another you.
One that had to always stay
a step behind.
One that could not be
"better"
than you.

Just for tonight,
let us pretend we have
no fears.
Just for this moment,
let us live right here.
Right now.
Just for tonight,
can we leave our
fears behind?

Please let me love the girl
that I spent years hating.
When I say I like my smile,
do not call me conceded.
When I say I am smart,
do not tell me I am
full of myself.
Please let me love the girl
I am because I have told
myself enough for
the both of us that
it was not true.

Who am I really?
I have to be someone
different for my friends.
Outgoing and funny,
or is that just pretend?
For everyone else,
I am focused on making
them proud.
But who am I really,
for myself?

She found beauty
in the way
the waves could
wipe the sand clean
of any past mistakes.

I HAVE TOO MANY
EXPECTATIONS AND THEY
ARE CONSTANTLY BEING
CRUSHED.
I HAVE TOO MANY
EXPECTATIONS AND
WHEN THEY DO
NOT HAPPEN
I GET MAD
AND LOST.

I did not even know what
my favorite color was
because I was too busy being
everyone else's
favorite color.

The same weekend I decided
I was going to start over.
Start fresh.
Was the same weekend it
poured and poured outside.
And that was no coincidence.

*-the rain brings a chance
to reset*

I am sorry I was a
no-call
no show
for the third time.
I do not know how to explain
what is going on in my mind.
I promise I am not making it up
even though I know you think I am
judging by the way you rolled
your eyes yet again.

I felt like the book
on the shelf that you
had every intention of
getting to,
but you just kept
looking past.
And with each new book
you brought home,
I knew I was becoming
more and more forgotten.
I just wanted you to
read me.
Understand me.
Please do not forget.

I have left so many tears at the
ocean that I started to wonder if
that is why it is saltwater.
Is the ocean filled with tears of
all the people who sit on the
coastline and spill their heart
and soul out into the unknown?

Do the stars look down on me
and question how I have
so much beauty and peace?
Because I am constantly looking up
to them and wondering just how
wonderful it must feel to be a
glimmer of light people look to.

My floorboards have felt my
anxiousness the most.
My feet pacing for hours
and hours.
Barefoot or in high heels.
My floorboards have felt my
anxiousness the most,
yet they still hold me up
time and time again.

I desire to still believe in
dreams and wishing
the same way I did when
I was young and
made wishes on pennies
thrown into
mall fountains.

It is easy to reel me back in
because I am always hoping this is
the time I will be enough.
Even after I have been thrown
overboard time and time again.
It is easy to reel me back in
because it is a safety net for me
to be with someone *anyone*
rather than alone.

I do not even know what,
I love you really means.
Other than being a bunch of
words you seem to
throw around with ease.

I know you do not hear my anxiety
or see my anxiety,
even when you are
right next to me.
But come inside my mind for a
while and you will see
all I have to do to act
so calm.
So at peace.
You will quickly learn,
it is nowhere near easy.

I was constantly chasing
people who could run
a marathon with ease.
I was constantly chasing
people who made me think they
would never leave.
But as soon as I was not
looking they got a head start that
I could never compete with.
They were always quick.
They were always swift.
They were bluffing.

Sorry for the fingerprints
I have left on your window.
I was chasing raindrops
down the glass.
I am so used to having to catch
the falling droplets before they
fall to the ground and collapse.

I messed up here.
I will leave and start over.
I messed up there.
I will leave and start over.
Burning bridges as I go.
Making it so I can
never come back.
I need to stop messing up
because now the places I have
messed up at are starting to link
with the places I want to go.
I have to start building
bridges.

There are playlists I will repeat
forever and ever.
From that summer.
That beach.
Our beautiful weather.
Even after we have long departed
from each other,
you will still find me pressing
play while the lyrics
pull us back together.

I WANT TO BE STILL,
BUT I NEED THE EARTH
TO BE STILL WITH ME.
SHE KEEPS SPINNING
NO MATTER WHAT.

Life is not dropping bread crumbs
leading me to where I am
supposed to go.
I have to bake my own bread
and make my own way, because
I will never learn if I am
handed everything.

I am trying to pull myself
out of a dark well.
I do not know how I will get
out, but I can see the light
so I know there is a way.
There is a way.
I will try with
all my might.

It is not about who is *only* at the
finish line to cheer you on.
It is about who is on the
sidelines along the way
when you have yet to be
victorious, but they still believe
you will get there.

There are only so many
weekends you can live for,
summers you can wait for,
and winters you can
beg to end,
before all you are doing is
wishing through life.
Have you stopped to love
today or are you already
dreaming of all the
next times?

I am leaving with very few things
and little knowledge of
where I am going,
but I will find my way
and figure out the details
as I go.
Nothing can surprise me
at this point.
Nothing is scarier to me right now
than not doing anything at all.

TABLE NO.	PERSONS	SERVER NO.		
13	1	2363-19		
BEV · APPET · SOUP/SALAD · ENTREE · VEG · DESSERT				
1 choc. milkshake				
side of fries				
FINDING				
MY				
WAY				

There is something to be said
about a diner that never has a
closing or an opening.
A place that is welcoming
when you have nowhere else to go.
With people who are eager to chat
or willing to leave you alone.
Where the food can range from
really good to really bad.
Yet somehow a 10:00 p.m. milkshake
will taste great no matter what,
and a 7:00 a.m. black coffee that
is a little burnt still tastes
like home.

I found myself while lost.
Somewhere in the middle of
a wrong turn
and a bad choice.
Losing who I thought
I was meant to be,
but really I found
my true voice.

Do not let go of hope.
She needs you.
She wants you.
She is a little shy,
but once she knows
she can trust that you
will not let her go.
Her light will come
shining through.

I stopped letting
others' opinions
take the driver's seat
for my life.
They can either be
a supportive passenger,
or find another ride.

There is happiness waiting
out there for you.
Clothed in your favorite color.
Smelling of nostalgia.
Looking like a familiar face you
just can not put a name to.
And she will wait
and she will wait,
until you are ready
to greet her again.
Even if you only stay
for a cup of coffee
and a chat.
Or if you unpack your things,
stay awhile,
and relax.
She will wait and she will wait,
and she will never ask why.
She understands that she is not a
place you can 100% reside.

I do not need you to
call me **strong**
to know that I am not **weak.**
I can hear my strength
in my voice as I speak.
I can feel it as I lift
the burdens off my own back.
I am strong.
I am worthy.
And the person who I need to
hear it from most is **me.**

The sunshine came for me on an
unexpected day.
It was not summertime
or warm outside.
The rays hit my face
on a cold afternoon
in the middle of March.
And I realized things
were going to be alright.
Even if alright was just today.
That was a start.

THESE HARD TIMES MAY
SEEM FOREVER, BUT ONE
DAY THIS WILL BE THE
PAST YOU THANK
FOR MAKING
YOU BETTER.

Alone is sometimes all
I need to be.
Eyes closed.
Mind open.
Sipping iced coffee
between the silence
and the breeze.
Alone does not have to
mean lonely.

Kiss those stars goodnight.
They will still shine for you
while you sleep.
Do not worry that they will be
gone come morning.
They are still there.
They are just giving the sun her
moment to shine alone.

Lost above the clouds,
or found beneath the trees.
I am a dreamer who is
still learning to live presently.

I saved all the flowers
you gave me in a coffee mug
on my table.
You laughed when you saw it,
as you pushed my hair
behind my ear.
And you pointed to my
makeshift vase and said,
"that is YOU right there."

I live through dream-filled eyes.
I see the birds
flying high with ease.
I see the flowers
blowing in the breeze.
I see the river moving to a beat.
Everything happening so
effortlessly.
My dream-filled eyes are not as
crazy as they seem.
I can dream out loud.

Find me driving down
the pacific northwest coastline,
in a VW wagon that fits me
just right.
Find me with my head
out the window.
Sun-kissed hair
blowing in the breeze.
As I look on at the contrast
of the orange sunset
and the blue sea.
Find me replaying this moment
in my mind.
The simple things in life.
This minimalistic time.

I will not forget who you were.
Not completely anyway.
There is still a piece of you
with me everywhere I go.
I did not hate who you were,
I just needed to move on to what
would bring me joy
and feed my dreaming soul.
So to the girl I left on the beach
that cloudy morning,
I just want you to know that
the new version of yourself is
doing much better than okay.
She feels less alone
more and more each day.

Loving yourself
is a do it yourself project
that you will not regret.

One day you will say,
"I made it.
I am great.
I am better than okay."
And that one day?
That one day
can start today.

Your star is a speck
in a constellation of many,
but that does not mean
that you shine any less.

I was a flower
plucked from my garden
and stuck in a vase
on your table
so you could
control my growth.
I still found a way
to bloom.

When the hour changes
from 11:59 p.m.
to 12:00 a.m.
I am thankful
to breathe in another day.
Whether the sun comes out
or not,
I am blessed
with another 12:00 AM
and that means a lot.

I can shine for myself.
I do not need you to
light the candle in me.
I am sunshine,
starlight,
fireflies,
and the moon.
I am the fire on the beach
lighting up the sand and the
conversations in bloom.
I was afraid to confidently say
that I am shining,
but not anymore.

Will I tell my children the
stories about how I did not
take that trip or risk?
Will they sit eagerly around the
fire to listen to stories that do
not have a cliff hanger
or plot twist?
After all, the good stories
are the ones that have a rough
patch that meets the turning point
and finds a happy ending.
So on the days I am stressing
about where I am,
I remember to think about the
stories I want to tell.
How yes they come with battles,
but they have
victories as well.

It was really all the places
in between where I was from
and where I was going
that taught me strength
and gave me just what I was
in need of.

One day you are going to tell me,
"Get in the car,
I have a surprise for you."
"What is it?" I will excitedly
but anxiously ask *(can't forget*
anxiety).
You will blindfold me and drive.
I will try to peak out the sides
(anxiety again).
I will smell fresh flowers
and wet grass.
I will hear birds
and the breeze.
You will ask,
"Are you ready?"
I will simply nod my head in a
yes, maybe, no kind of way.
You will take off the blindfold
and there in front of me will be a
house surrounded by willow trees.
A door will be painted a wild red
like we always wanted.
We will be home.
No more wandering.

IT IS NOT ABOUT _IF_.
LET _IF_ GO.
IT IS _WHEN_ THAT YOU
WILL WANT TO
HOLD ON TO.

At the end of the day
there is still light
eager to pour through.
The darkness has
a spotlight.
Do not forget about
the moon.

To my five-year-old self with
dream-filled eyes,
I am sorry I let those amazing
ideas of yours drift from my mind.
I spent the time searching
for them again,
when I stopped buying into
the lies.
To my five-year-old self who had
no problem believing in herself,
I have my confidence back and it
is not leaving.

To all the girls I used to be.
The ghosts of the old me.
Please stop lingering.
I do not want you back in my mind.
I do not want to be friends.
The girl I am now is someone I
want to stay close with
until the end.
I am grateful for
what you taught me,
but I am ready to put those
relationships to rest.

Today I am loving myself
as I come.
I am not trying to turn
myself into someone
I wish I was.
The woman I woke up as today
has more than enough to give.
Does she have room
for improvement?
Of course.
But that does not mean
she is not still amazing
as she comes.
Start your morning thanking
yourself for who you are
right now.

I want to collaborate
like the sun and rain
do for our beautiful nature.
I do not want to compete
like animals that think
the other is going to
bring danger.

It is hard to start over.
Go back to square one.
Especially when you
were so close to done.
It is hard to start over.
Travel back to the line.
But it will be well worth it
so you can learn and grow
all you need to this time.

You can sit and wait
for the weather to get better.
Look out the window.
Complain it is dreary.
Or you can get out,
dance in the rain,
and get ready to chase the sun
when it comes.

I promise when I
invite you over for dinner,
you are at a table
that is eager to welcome you.
Come as you are.
There is no dress code.
No requirement to talk.
Do not worry about how much food
you do or do not eat.
This is a table to come 100%
as who you feel you are.
Do not hold back.
Please come.
I want to cheers to
who you are
and who you hope to
embrace more of.

What song will play for you
as you drive off into the sunset
you always dreamt of?
The sunset that is
your dream come true.
The reds,
yellows,
and bright blues.
What anthem will be there
to play for you,
like you are the closing scene
in that feel-good movie?

I am taking back my power
to write the story
I want to tell.
I will no longer allow
someone else to write
my story for me.
They do not know my plots
or turning points.
They do not know
who I am beyond
who they think they are
for me.

Getting lost taught me
I have survival skills
I did not even know about.
I may not be able to
fight off a bear,
but I can ignore
hateful things
coming out
of your mouth.

I am the tree you will
come back to in five years
look at and say,
*"Oh, how much you have grown while
I was away."*

—I can flourish on my own

I HAD TO STOP SAYING
YES ALL OF THE TIME
IN ORDER TO GET TO
WHERE I WANTED
TO GO THIS
TIME.

"Wow, I did not even
recognize her."
"Who?" You ask.
As I look in the mirror
with gold trim
I see a girl with a
red lipstick smile
and glee in her eyes.
"Me." I say.
"I have not truly
seen her in a while."

You are the flower I see
budding in a garden
only filled with weeds.
Push through your limitations
and show yourself that
you have had the power
all along to grow
no matter where you
start from.

Every single day
I pictured doing one thing
I was always afraid to do.
Every single day
I would tell myself
that one day
I am going to face this fear
and make my victory
from it come true.
Over and over
I would replay it
in my head.
Even if the only time
my victory happened
was for that five minutes
each morning as
I closed my eyes
and laid in bed.

I never doubted that
the sun would rise
come morning
or set come night.
I want to carry that
assurance with me
for everything
in my life.

Without the behind the scenes
work from the roots,
a flower would never bloom.

It may hard to not be all the
people that everyone else
would like you to be.
But only you know what
your soul needs.
Keep that in mind.
Listen to your heart.
Listen to what people
have to say,
but do not allow them
to steer your life
in a direction you know you
would never want to take.

I am trusting that today's
struggles are tomorrow's
victories.
I am trusting there is
some reason all of this is
happening to me.

Although I have mountains
and deserts ahead I know there is
that lake view with tall red pine
trees and crystal clear water.
That is what is getting me through
these harder times.
Knowing that soon I will
be diving into the water and
reflecting on it all.

The best decision I ever made was
waking up early,
greeting the fresh air,
sipping my coffee,
and having my phone nowhere near.
The best decision I ever made was
waking up early and not letting
the internet be my escape.

I want to thank failure.
You taught me resilience.
You taught me to hope.
But most importantly
you taught me that things
will not always go my way.
Failure is growth.

I will carry my body through
raindrops and thunder.
I will carry my body through
sun rays and cool breezes.
I will carry my body through
lots of different weather.
But I am still standing after
it all.

I was always scared
to tell myself
I love you,
because every time
I heard
it before,
they never meant it.
And I wanted to mean it.

People will jump to conclusions
about you.
People will label you how
they see fit.
People will create their own ideas
about who you are.
People who do this are the ones
that are not content with who
they are, so they worry more about
who *you* are instead.

I used to hate my thighs.
I would say they looked
like cottage cheese.
Then one day as I stood at the
mirror, I thanked my thighs for
holding me up all these years.
Even with all the hate
I tossed their way,
they still supported me
every single day.

She follows her intuition.
Planting seeds with no doubt
they will grow.
Willing to open it up as a
community garden,
because she never wants someone
to feel alone.

Five years from today,
even a year from today,
I will look back and thank
who I am today.
Even if I may not be best friends
with her right now,
in the future I will be thanking
her for how strong she made it
through that hell.

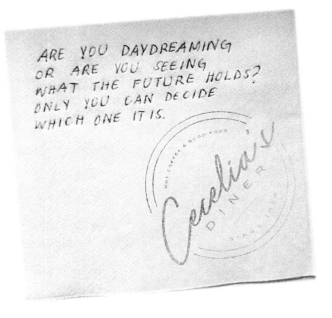

Your pain is 100% real
even if no one else
understands it.
It is not their pain to get,
because they are not the ones
feeling it.

When everything is going just
right, take it is a sign.
Do not question if it is just a
coincidence this time.

I will no longer
call myself a mess.
Yes, I have papers scattered.
There is a coffee mug tower
in the sink.
The mail looks like I have been
out of town for weeks.
But this is the first time
I am happy,
even if my house may not
look like it.
Just because my house
is put together
does not always mean I feel
put together inside the body I
call home.

How many storms have you hunkered
down for and still come out of
just fine?
How many times have you been lost
in the woods and still found your
way out in time?
Things are going to be alright.

Yes, everything comes to an end
but an end is really just the
beginning of all the
opportunities ahead.

I took my broken heart
and fixed it on my own.
It is not perfectly put back
together, but it is done with
the same love as a child's
arts and craft project
they eagerly bring home.

Today if you do
nothing else at all,
at least take a moment
to stand tall.
Take a deep breath.
Put your hand on your chest.
Feel your heartbeat.
Feel the air move
through your lungs.
You are beautifully alive.
You are needed here so much.

The courage you see in me
is years and years
of fighting with my anxiety.
I still get scared to
face it at times,
but I will fight and fight for it
to not control my life.
I will fight
and I will fight.

I no longer tiptoe around people
who once intimidated me.
I walk past them confidently.
I started to realize that they
were not threatening at all.
They are as human as I am.
They have insecurities,
they trip,
and they fall.

You are not weak for asking for
help from another.
Some days we need support more
than others.

This world may seem
too crowded for you
to make your mark,
but millions of stars
still fit in the sky
and shine like they are
the only one doing so.

-Shine like you are the only one

In a world striving for
perfection,
be unique.
In a world that wants
flawless,
be you.

I HAVE LEFT THE WORDS
I WISH I COULD SAY
ON NAPKINS ACROSS
THE WHOLE COUNTRY.

— I HOPE THEY
BRING YOU
COMPANY

Every person will not be your
person,
and they do not need to be.
That is why there are so many
people on this earth.
Find the people you can
count on.
The people who care
deeply for you.
Do not worry about pleasing
everyone.
It is an exhausting task you will
never have enough time to get
through.

It was a long road to get here,
but I am so glad I did not make
that U-turn I wanted to take
300 miles back.
Oh, all I would have missed.
Oh, all the growth
I would have lacked.

One morning I woke up and I caught
a glimpse of her in the mirror.
I felt her as I struggled to get
out of bed in the morning.
I heard her as I sat on the couch
staring blankly at the wall.
And all I could think was,
she is back.
But I handled her well.
I addressed that she was there.
Allowed myself to feel
the emotions she brought me.
Eventually, I felt her slowly
going away more and more.
Maybe she will come back
again someday,
but I am ready to handle her.

-when anxiety comes back

Each night before I would
close my eyes to rest,
he would call and ask me to list
five things I love
about myself best.
At first it would take me
an hour.
Sometimes two.
Why was thinking up things I love
about myself so hard to do?
But as we kept doing this month
after month,
I started being able to list what
I love in under 30 seconds.
Then one night as we were doing
our normal routine I said to him,
*"Who knew I would one day be
saying what I love about myself
faster than you."*
"I did." He said.
*"I always believed it was
something you could do."*

Eating in front of other people
would make me nervous.
Feeling the need to justify why I
am eating what I was eating.
Reasons popping in my head of what
I would say about why it was okay.
I have not had much to eat today,
so I deserve it.
I ate healthy yesterday, **so I**
deserve it.
I do not eat junk food often, **so I**
deserve it.
When I really owe no one an
explanation.
I deserve to eat in peace.

I am trying to become more like
that fearless girl I was
when I was young.
The one who said she would
go on *Fear Factor* and eat worms
without a problem,
or lay in a bed of snakes
effortlessly.
I am trying to become more like
that fearless girl I was
when I was young.
The one most would call naive.

Every side is your good side.
Photograph all your beauty.

As I cleaned out my closet
for the third time this year,
I was met face to face with the
jeans I promised I would
fit in for years.
That size I wanted to
so badly squeeze in.
Even if it made a ripping noise
and pop, off goes the button.
As I cleaned out my closet for the
third time this year,
I finally put those jeans in a
giveaway bag and told myself no
more hating the body
I have right here.

The most empowering thing I did for myself was when I stopped doubting my abilities even when everyone else interjected their negative opinion of my positive choices.

No one will care about your dream
more than you.
No one will work harder for
your dream more than you.
You are in the driver seat of your
dream and if you do not push the
gas, you will not get far.
Because no one is going to pick up
your dream in their car.

When I told you all of my dreams
late at night through the phone,
instead of telling me I was crazy,
you whispered back,
"Dream bigger."
And for once I felt seen.
For once I was not alone.

I CAN BE FEARLESS
AND STILL CRY.
THAT DOES NOT MAKE
MY FEARLESSNESS
ANY LESS MINE.

Releasing my need
to always be right.
Allowing myself to accept
when I am wrong.
This is something that
took me far too long.
But how freeing it feels.
How right it feels to admit
my wrongs.

I got tired of being the girl
who never would forgive.
I got tired of remembering
all of my grudges.
Give grace.
Give grace.
Give grace.
It is what you would want
someone to do for you too.

Go for your dreams at whatever
pace you would like.
Run,
skip,
or walk.
Go for your dreams at whatever
pace you would like.
Some dreams take time.

You reminded me of honey,
because you stuck around long
after you were gone.
And cleaning up after you
was not a simple task.
You left your mark.
You left your trash.

That stranger may wonder why I
smiled so big at them as I passed,
but I remember what it was like to
walk by people and wish all they
did was at least acknowledge me.
Maybe we are all moving too fast.

Stick a postcard in the mail with
an encouraging line or two.
Send it off to a friend.
You never know what that
small gesture may do.

All my smiles may look the same,
but my brain can recognize all the
ones that are real and all the
ones that are fake.

Who thought I would love
the rain when I used to only
crave the nice weather.
But then I realized how much the
rain is looked down upon when all
it is trying to do is bring
nourishment and
make things better.

It is ok to let go of places
only disguised as home.
Hit the road and roam.
It is your life.
Do not fear taking control.

I will try and
I will try
to bottle my happiness up
like sand from the ocean.
Place it on a shelf within reach.
So even as time passes I can
open it up and remember how
I felt mid-June,
with eagerness in my eyes
under the full moon.

I thought I was lost
all of the time,
but really it was
just people telling me
I was lost because where
I was did not align
with where they wanted me
to be.

I wonder how different you would
feel if the same attention you
gave to the surface of your body
each morning, was the same
attention you gave to your soul.

-your soul wants your care too

I hope all the encouragement
I give you sticks like
fingerprints on a
clean window.
I hope it lingers.
I hope you do not want to
pull out the glass cleaner
for awhile.

I LAID DOWN AND LOOKED
UP AT THE STORMY SKIES
AND SAID,
"YOU WILL NOT TAKE
ME DOWN. THIS
IS MY FIGHT."

How long will we keep calling
confidence cockiness?
How long will we keep tearing
people down
but then complain that
they are too insecure?

Do not be afraid
to tell your story.
Do not think your story
is going to be boring.
There is no exact
story like yours.
Your story wants to
be heard.
Someone out there
needs it.

I was waiting for someone to stop
and ask me,
"Hey, are you actually ok?"
But instead I stopped myself as I
looked into the river bed and
said,
*"I know you are not ok. What can I
do for you? How can I make you
feel better?"*
Sometimes I need to hear it more
from myself than others.

Where will you go?
What is next?
That is the fun part,
it is your story so you get to
decide how you want to
tell the rest of it.

I know you prefer to
tiptoe around and hope
no one notices you.
But do not be afraid
to tread with footprints
that fall deep into the ground.
Do not be afraid to
leave your mark here.

I would ask you what you
looked for in someone you were
attracted to.
Then I let that be
the guidelines to how
I would be.
Not anymore.
Not anymore.
I know I will find someone who
truly loves ME.

I would like to thank all the
random pieces of paper,
the napkins and receipts,
for being the one consistent
thing in my life that absorbs
every word I say.
The good and the bad
with absolutely no judgment.

This is not my,
now she lives
happily ever after.
This is my,
now she lives in a way she can
recognize what makes her
happy after all.

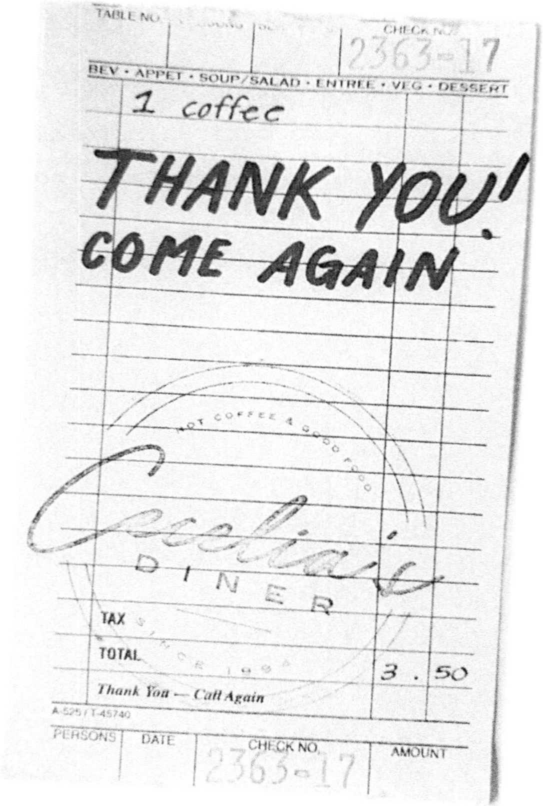
TABLE NO.
CHECK NO.
2363-17
BEV • APPET • SOUP/SALAD • ENTREE • VEG • DESSERT
1 coffee
THANK YOU!
COME AGAIN
HOT COFFEE & GOOD FOOD
DINER
TAX
TOTAL
3.50
Thank You — Call Again
PERSONS
DATE
CHECK NO.
2363-17
AMOUNT

~

To my dreamers,

Thank you for the beautiful
support you give me.
I am honored each time
you read my poems,
share them with a friend,
or write them as a reminder to
yourself.
You motivate me to keep sharing
my journey.

~

To read more work by Jennae Cecelia, check out her other five books:

Bright Minds Empty Souls

Uncaged Wallflower

Uncaged Wallflower- Extended Edition

I Am More Than a Daydream

I Am More Than My Nightmares

Dear Me at Fifteen

About the author

www.JennaeCecelia.com

@JennaeCecelia on Instagram

Jennae Cecelia is a best-selling author of inspirational poetry books and is best known for her book, Uncaged Wallflower.

She is also an ins speaker who digs into topics like self-love, self-care, mental health, and body positivity.

Her mission is to encourage people to reach their full potential and live a life filled with positivity and love.

Printed in Great Britain
by Amazon